An American Nightmare
The Pitfalls of Home Ownership

By

Toni R. Harris

www.TotalPublishingAndMedia.com

Copyright © 2012 by Toni R. Harris

All rights reserved.

No part of this book may be reproduced, stored in a retrieval system, or transmitted by any means, electronic, mechanical, photocopying, recording, or otherwise, without written permission from the author.

ISBN: 978-1-937829-00-1

The thoughts related in this book are related to house rentals vs. apartment rentals, which is another subject entirely

What People Are Saying

American Nightmare: The Pitfalls of Home Ownership

Home ownership – American Dream or Nightmare! After all a nightmare is a dream, right? How many of us grew up in a generation where we were "expected" to own our home with a fence, a yard, some kids and a "happy ever after" dream life. When in reality, home ownership has its down sides, too. Toni Harris shares her own personal stories of owning a home and the buyer's remorse that she suffered. She reminds us that you can't take back a house just because you don't like it after the first few months. So, she cautions, do you homework! Make sure the time is right for you, for the real estate market and for the area where you are selecting a home. Read this book. Ask questions! Do your homework – as you should with any major purchase! You get to choose and you accept the consequences of your choice! American Dream or American Nightmare! It's up to you.

Sandy Lawrence
Perceptive Marketing
Publicist

The American Nightmare is a quick study in the obstacles and problems faced when considering buying a home in today's economy. It gives the reader something to think about and a different perspective to contemplate. The true story from the author's experience totally substantiates the difficulties that may be encountered. Enjoyable read!

Joyce Jenkins
Computer Consultant & Newspaper Editor

Toni Harris'AnAmerican Nightmare – The Pitfalls of Home Ownership was liberating for me. As a "baby boomer," it was drilled into my head that the measurement of my success was determined by my address. So you can imagine the guilt I felt when I lost my house to foreclosure several years ago. This book literally set me free from that guilt.

Sharon Jenkins
Literary Coach and Editor
Authorpreneurship

Growing up as a woman I had this dream of Prince Charming, white picket fences, a couple of kids and maybe a dog. When it didn't happen that way for me, I hopped on the bandwagon to achieve as much of that dream as possible on my own and bought a home. Behind that dream are real-life issues, like yards I don't know how to cultivate, pests, garbage disposals gone rogue, and hoses that break on your toilet leaving your "dream" a wet-soggy mess with very little options. As a single woman, take it from me, home ownership ain't all it's cracked up to be!

Nakia Laushaul
Author, Running from Solace
www.nakiarlaushaul.com

An American Nightmare, is a reality check for both the potential and existing homeowner. Toni addresses the truth as it relates to owning a home. As a homeowner who has experienced the challenges of being a landlord, and not being able to sell when our life changed, it is imperative for readers to understand that there are risks associated with being a homeowner especially in a down economy.

Pat Tucker
Journalist/Author of Party Girl

Dedication

This book is dedicated to all of the families whose American dream turned into a nightmare.

Acknowledgements

I would like to acknowledge a few people who helped me to complete the Nightmare Book.

To my author coach and editor, Sharon Jenkins, I could not have completed this project without you. To my mother and friend, Joyce Jenkins, *I'm grateful for your eternal support*. No matter what bright idea I come up with you are always there to support me. To my children, Morgan & Garrett, I know life has not been *easy the past few years,* but the future is looking bright. Last but not least, my husband, Robert, thank you for your encouragement, support and seeing my vision. I love you all very much.

Table of Contents

Chapter 1 - Now's the Time to Buy 1

Chapter 2 - The Second Time Around 5

Chapter 3 - It ALL Comes Crashing Down 9

Chapter 4 - History of Home Ownership 14

Chapter 5 - Psychology of Home Ownership....... 19

Chapter 6 - The Real Cost of Ownership............. 27

Chapter 7 - Understanding Mortgages 41

Chapter 8 - Solutions... 51

TONI HARRIS is a passionate, dynamic and energetic speaker who "wows" audiences across the country, melding best practices with real world solutions. Toni never meets a stranger and is eager to motivate others to reach their full potential. Her transparency and ability to  connect with the audience allows her to bring out the best in people, helping them develop critical skills and deliver bottom line results.

Toni is no stranger to risk, change and adversity. At 23 years old Toni took her first career risk, leaving her job in the oil and gas industry to become a business owner. In 2000, she took another leap of faith, relocating to Florida to become a financial advisor in the middle of what turned out to be the worst stock market America had ever experienced. Utilizing techniques and strategies outlined in her programs, Toni was able to re-evaluate, recover and move forward to become a well-respected, top performer in her industry.

Unfortunately, life has not been a bed of roses and Toni, like many Americans, has experienced the pangs of home ownership. As a result of her experience, she wants to educate hard working Americans about the pitfalls of home ownership before it's too late. She also wants her audience to know it is okay to be a financially smart renter and not fall into the trap of owning a home because everyone else is doing it.

Professional

Toni is also an independent financial advisor. As an advisor Toni handled financial and retirement planning for several large employers in the Houston area. She has managed over 1,000 clients with over $50 million in assets. She currently holds the following licenses:

* Series 6 – Investment Company & Variable Contracts Rep
* Series 7 – General Securities Rep
* Series 24 – General Securities Registered Principal
* Series 51 – Municipal Securities Limited Principal
* Series 66 – Investment Advisory Rep
* Life/Health/Variable Annuity Ins. – FL, TX

Education

* Currently pursuing a Bachelor of Science degree in Business Management with a concentration in Small Business and Entrepreneurship at the University of Phoenix

Personal

* Married to Robert P. Powell, Jr., head bowling coach at Texas Southern University
* She has two adult children, Garrett and Morgan
* For fun, Toni likes to get together with girlfriends, attend the theatre and concerts, walking and curling up with a good novel.

Alamo Asset Advisors is the operating name for Alamo Investment Advisors, LLC, an independently owned Registered Investment Advisor. Toni Harris is a registered representative of WFG. Securities offered through WFG Investments, Inc. WFG member FINRA and SIPC.

Contributors

Godiva Anderson, Realtor

Godiva has been a REALTOR for 14 years. She began her career as an assistant to a top producer to a broker-owner in two states. She is the broker/owner of Godiva Real Estate Company in Louisiana. Currently resides in Houston, where she is in the process of opening Godiva Ensemble of Acquisitions. Godiva is very passionate about her real estate career and the relationships of her clients. Servant at heart, Godiva volunteers for several nonprofits and sits on the board of directors of one. She has consulted clients with their best interests in mind.

Karla Dennis, Tax Advisor

Karla is a licensed Enrolled Agent through the US Treasury Department which allows her to practice in all 50 states. She has over 25 years experience as a tax professional. She has an undergraduate degree in accounting and a master's degree in taxation. She considers herself a tax guru. She loves what she does and is passionate about helping others realize there are advantages to using the tax code. Karla is the CEO of Cohesive which is a Tax Consultancy and Business Advisory Firm in Cypress, California. She has clients all over the United States. Her practice consists of 17 full time employees dedicated to helping their clients.

Shantel Landry, Mortgage Broker

Shantel has been a mortgage broker for 12 years and is passionate about the real estate industry. She has over ten years experience in the banking, finance, mortgage and lending industry with a focus on business management. Shantel is a common law notary public officer for the State of Texas and is a previous business partner of a nationwide company in the real-estate industry connecting with multiple companies and providing centralized solutions. She developed an exchange adeptness to expedite streamline processes through expert service excellence. Shantel is a member of local network groups where she shares ideas, gains new business and marketing skills, provides support and motivation and stimulates the growth of business opportunities.

Foreword

During my 18 years in the mortgage and real estate industry, serving in a multitude of roles from Realtor to Loan officer, trainer, manager and even compliance officer, I witnessed directly and indirectly, thousands of home purchases. One of my most vivid memories was one specific year where there were approximately 7 new constructions occurring at the same time. By the time they were all completed, I saw 3 divorces, a builder sued and an intermediary brought in to help solve the builder/borrower conflicts. This occurred well before the financial crisis that began in 2007 started. And this is only a small glimpse from my 18 years in the industry. With all of the financial challenges that were created or amplified from the current crisis, I made a career shift and now work with families and individuals who need help reducing or eliminating their debt and help restoring and maintaining their credit.

Many books have been written on the benefits of homeownership. Toni takes a bold step and presents a look at the other side; the pitfalls, problems and 'nightmares' of homeownership. She relates it through her personal experience and helps you think through the real reasons you should buy, *or not buy*, a home. As Toni shares her experiences into the world of homeownership your eyes will be opened to the realities and how to not let the emotions of the 'dream' of homeownership dominate your decisions. By maintaining a balance of logic, emotion and guidance from a truly competent professional, your life will be greatly improved whether you buy a home or not. Toni does an excellent job of presenting the problems, showing the psychology of, and true costs of owning a home. Then she guides you through what you need to do to make the best decision in determining if buying is right for you and if so, the process involved so you don't live the 'nightmare' she lived.

Here is the good news. If you follow this story and the guidance that Toni provides in this book, the odds of experiencing your own homeownership nightmare will be drastically reduced. One of the most profound moments in my life in the mortgage industry occurred at the baby shower of my only child who we adopted at birth. As I looked around the room I saw something I had never realized before; 80% of the people in that room were friendships developed as a result of them buying a home with my guidance. It was a great, and very emotional moment for me. These friends did *not* have a 'nightmare' experience. May the same be true for you!

Darrel Cunningham, Money Coach
DCStrategies
Tulsa, OK

Chapter 1

Now's the Time to Buy

"My dad called today," my husband, Brandon, said to me. "Oh really, what did he say?" I replied. He said he thinks it's time for us to buy a house and he wants to help with the down payment. I thought to myself, sounds good, but I'm not sure I'm ready to buy a house. We were living in an apartment and I was comfortable there. However, our son was a year old and everyone was telling us they thought we should have more space for our growing family. We knew we wanted at least one more child so buying a house seemed reasonable. Brandon's dad had owned apartment buildings and several homes so he really stressed the value of owning a home. The fact that he wanted to help with the down payment was also a great incentive, so we set out to find our new home.

It didn't take us long before we found our first home in Northwest Houston. It was a three bedroom, two bath, two car garage home. It was about 1,600 square feet and a great starter home. I remember when we first viewed the home, my toddler son ran around the vacant house like he belonged there. He was so excited and comfortable! We thought, this is it. We've found our new home. But, from the beginning the home was a disappointment to me. I remember Brandon and I had our first "real" fight over the house. The problem for me was at the onset, it was too much work. We had to clean, paint, and do minor repairs to make it move-in ready. After about a week, I disliked the house. Little did I know how much I would grow to hate the house.

I suffer from a syndrome called buyer's remorse. I'm glad the professionals put a name to it because I called it "chickenitis." Buyer's remorse is a condition many people suffer from. Anytime I make a major purchase, I initially regret it. I remember trying to return a car like it was a pair of shoes. The dealer laughed so hard at me. After this experience, I learned to do my homework really well when making a major purchase because the retailers don't just take back the items because I "changed my mind." So it was the same way with this house. About a week after we moved in, I remember telling my husband how miserable I was. We were making about $30,000 a year combined and we had just signed a mortgage for $50,000 (at the time, this amount of money seemed huge). I cried, pouted, and felt a lot of pressure. Then the

An American Nightmare: The Pitfalls of Home Ownership

maintenance started. I remember our first major maintenance project. A storm blew through and the wooden fence blew down. Like most young couples, we didn't have an emergency cash fund and I remember thinking how are we going to come up with the funds to make these repairs and pay the monthly mortgage? Fortunately, my mother was there to help, in fact, she often came to the rescue. Thank God for my mother.

"I hate this house," I said.

"Why?" Brandon asked.

"Because we don't have the money to do the maintenance and I can't even afford to put blinds on the windows or paint the walls. Look at the kitchen, it's dark and ugly. The drawer faces are starting to fall off," I replied. I didn't mention the barking dog from the neighbors who thought 3 a.m. was an ideal time to express himself. "I wish we didn't have this house." Brandon shook his head and proceeded to tell me how ungrateful I was and how I should appreciate owning a home. However, since I was the one who was responsible for paying the bills, he didn't really see the "real" cost of owning the home. I thought, if I was a renter, I wouldn't have to spend money on maintenance and I could just move to escape the annoying dog. To make a long story short, we stayed in the home for 10 years. One year prior to selling, we took

$20,000 out of Brandon's 401K to make some much needed repairs along with some remodeling. We replaced the kitchen cabinet door fronts, put down tile, carpeted, painted, wallpapered, and made some improvements outside. Really, for the first time, I actually began to like the house. In fact, when it was time to sell the home, it sold in less than a month because we had done such a good job in our improvements. I was proud of what we accomplished. When it was time to sell, we got the top price in the neighborhood. We sold the house for $73,000. Because we had refinanced around year 7, the balance was still at $50,000. After closing costs, realtor commissions and paying off the remaining balance, we walked away with $13,000. Did you hear me say, We spent $20,000 on home repairs, from an early withdrawal from our 401K? We did not even receive our money back for the repairs, let alone the interest, taxes, insurance, neighborhood association fees, maintenance, 401k taxes and penalty. So while we walked away with a lump sum of $13,000, the real cost over 10 years far exceeded the "profit" at the closing table. This was my first experience with home ownership. The experience was so much fun, we decided to do it again and again and again.

Chapter 2

The Second Time Around

The reason we sold our house in Houston was to relocate to Florida for me to become a financial advisor. We moved to Port St. Lucie (PSL), a city in south Florida. At the time, Port St. Lucie was the fastest growing city in Florida. We purchased a piece of land for $7,000. Had we bought it the year before, we would have paid $3,000. So the economy was doing very well. A friend recommended we check out his home builder. Port St. Lucie was booming with new home sales. I was excited because I always wanted a stucco home. I also wanted a new home where I picked all of the decorations right down to the faucets and light fixtures. We were able to purchase this 2,100 square foot home for only $113,000. We used $7,000 out of the $13,000 profit from the sale of our first house as a down payment. This house felt like a better deal than the house in Houston. I actually loved this house and I don't remember having buyer's remorse with this purchase.

However, I remember the maintenance expense of window coverings, painting, patio enclosure, landscaping, etc. The maintenance in the first year was astronomical. We probably spent over $10,000 in maintenance alone. Not to mention all the money we spent on decorating and making it mine. Still, I didn't regret buying this house.

St. Lucie County grew so fast they began to increase our taxes at a rapid pace. They needed the tax base to keep up with the infrastructure to accommodate their new population. Our property values also increased exponentially because the demand for housing was great. Many people relocated from the east coast and they were getting a deal on their homes. People were selling their homes in the east coast states and paying cash for their homes in PSL. The economy was booming and the home prices rose from $120,000 to over $300,000 in 3 years! Homeowners in droves were refinancing their homes and pulling out the equity. We were one of them. In early 2004, we refinanced to recapture some of our equity. I remember we received about $70,000 in cash from the home. Of course, we put about $20,000 of the funds back into the home, paid off some other debts including a car, probably took a vacation, I had major surgery and we paid some other miscellaneous items. Now, after closing costs, fees, taxes, etc. our mortgage was $200,000. This scenario is the good side of home ownership. Except, now the money is gone, which is okay since we accomplished some of our goals, but now we are paying more interest on a higher mortgage, and because the property was reappraised at the higher value, our taxes doubled. We are also now paying a higher payment because our escrow increased considerably.

Port St. Lucie wasn't the only place where the housing market was booming. The majority of the country was experiencing a great boom. There were more and more infomercials on how to buy homes with no money down. There were programs teaching people how to buy houses with tax liens, how to flip their homes, and how to buy foreclosures at auctions. There were so many "you can do it too" programs out there, the ordinary person with no real estate experience instantly became an overnight expert. To top it off, the mortgage industry got real creative with their mortgage instruments. There were subprime mortgages, interest only loans, variable loans with low introductory rates, no money down loans, and loans where you could buy a house which was 3-4 times the amount you could normally afford because of the creative lending practices. This created a perfect storm for the impending real estate crash.

Unfortunately, my husband thought this was a good time to enter the real estate investment game. In 2005, he quit his job to become a real estate investor and landlord. Being a good wife, I needed to stand by my man, right? Because he didn't have a job, he used my income and credit, which was over 750 to acquire these creative loans. Now remember, I have buyer's remorse really bad. So every loan I signed for felt a little like a slow death to me. But because he had been supportive of me when I started my career as a financial advisor, I felt I needed to be unselfish and help him grow his business. I now realize his support was moral and emotional, not financial. I should have put on my short skirt, grabbed my pom-poms, shook my behind and cheered him on to success. I should not have given him my financial support. Hindsight is truly 20/20.

Chapter 3

It <u>ALL</u> Comes Crashing Down

Our first investment home was literally the house next door. Our neighbors had to move unexpectedly, so we purchased their home. This was in 2005 when Florida experienced two hurricanes, Frances and Jeanne, within two weeks of each other. We were fortunate because neither of our homes experienced damage but several others did. Our first renter was a dream. She was displaced because of the storms and rented from us with six months rent upfront! This landlord thing wasn't looking too bad. As you can imagine, this situation didn't last long. After her six months were up, she moved back to her home and we were left to find the next renters. In the meantime, the market was starting to slow down. The house stayed vacant for a month and then we found our next renters. Unfortunately, to compete and get someone in there quickly we leased it for $200 less than the monthly mortgage. To top it off, the tenants were less than ideal and they were consistently late with the rent. We were getting in over our heads.

In late 2006, the real estate market all over the United States, but particularly in Florida, came to a screeching halt. I remember my husband saying, it's just a slowdown, things will turn around. He continued buying properties and spending money remodeling properties he had already bought. He had begun to associate with other real estate investors and they were telling him to keep doing what he was doing. I remember vividly, like it was yesterday, sitting at the closing table for the last house we purchased. I did not want to sign. I told him it was a bad idea. He had a plan. He was going to flip this house to someone who was already ready to buy. I had tears streaming down my face because I knew it was not a good deal but he was committed to the seller and I was committed to him. So in support of my husband, kicking and screaming and literally crying, I signed.

BIG MISTAKE! The committed, sure buyer backed out and we couldn't sell it. So I began to pay the mortgage on this home which was not our homestead. Remember, he did not have a job and I was financially carrying the bulk of the household bills plus this house where the mortgage was $1,400 a month. This note, coupled with the rental house really put a great deal of stress on our marriage.

One day Brandon came to me and said he wanted to ask our 70 year old neighbor to invest in his latest housing project. This was a house he had purchased without my knowledge because seeing where the market was going and having my pulse on the economy, he pretty much knew I was done buying houses. I was emphatic. "Do not ask her for money," I told him.

"Do not ask her for money." I told him. "You know how she is about her money." She had experienced her own success in buying property in Port St. Lucie during the "boom" and had the money available. She was by no means destitute and she was very sharp, but I didn't want to be indebted to her. I repeated, "Do not ask her for money."

Brandon began working on this last house. I thought he was putting too much money into the house but he insisted he had to spend the funds to get it ready to sell. To this day, I have no idea how much he spent on this project or where the money came from because by now he was working part-time making about $700 per month, none of which came into the household to help me carry the bills and the additional houses. The resentment and anger began to build.

Toni R. Harris

In April 2007, I received a voice message from my neighbor. "Toni", she said in her thick Jamaican accent, "I've been calling Brandon and he has been ignoring my calls. He owes me a lot of money and he won't pay me back. He won't return my calls or let me know what's going on. I need you to call me and let me know how *you* are going to take care of what he owes me." Unfortunately for Brandon, he was home. I played the message for him. Now, whenever Brandon was caught, he would just have this dumb, "I got my hand stuck in the cookie jar kind of look." He stared at me. I asked him, "How much do you owe her?" He hung his head and said $17,000. I later found out from her it was more like $30,000. Now I know where the money to fix the house came from. I hit the ceiling. "Didn't we discuss this?" I asked you not to take her money and you did it anyway and now she wants me to pay her back. I was not a part of the deal and I'm not paying her a dime!" The financial stress was mounting and pulling us apart. To top it off, Brandon had diabetes and high blood pressure and his health was suffering because of the financial strain. I also began to notice he would sit and stare into space for long periods of time. It was like he was paralyzed. In hindsight, I realize he was slipping into a depression, but at the time, I was too consumed with the financial strain to notice.

In June 2007, I left my husband. I figured, I can do bad all by myself. Since I was carrying the entire financial load, I decided to vacate the marriage. Again, hindsight is 20/20 and if I had it to do again, I would not have left my marriage, especially after the events in the months to follow. Brandon became so dependent on me, he didn't know how to function alone. By the time our divorce was final in February 2008, he had suffered a mild heart attack. Subsequently, he returned to work returned to work at his previous employer full-time. As a result of the divorce, he was awarded all of the houses, including our homestead, and was to having them all transferred to him. Of course, the mortgage companies wanted to know if he was qualified to handle all of the mortgages and if he was income or credit worthy. So what did he do? Nothing. He never transferred the mortgages to his name and they all foreclosed under my name. I would go after him today, but he passed away suddenly from diabetes and high blood pressure complications after losing his job and health insurance. Frankly, the stress and pressure of our failed eighteen year marriage, owing several people thousands of dollars and his failing health were all factors in his demise. A very, very sad situation.

Chapter 4

History of Home Ownership

From the time I was able to understand money, I have always heard people say, "You have to own a home." "Don't rent and pay someone else's mortgage; get your piece of the American dream." So home ownership was instilled into most of us at an early age. In this chapter, we will address the following questions:

- How did home ownership become the American dream?
- Where did this mentality of "everyone needs to own a home" come from?
- How did immigration and certain rights play a part in owning a home?

Home ownership dates back to the early 1800's right after the founding of the United States of America. All of the signers of the Declaration of Independence were land owners and were given special rights including voting privileges because

An American Nightmare: The Pitfalls of Home Ownership

they owned the land. As the early settlers began to move West, they claimed the land as their own and began to "settle" in, moving out anyone who was in their way, namely the Native Americans. At this time, America was an agricultural economy and the land owners used their land to amass their fortunes. This looked very attractive to non-landowners. So the unwritten "dream" is that everyone should own land that they can call their own and turn it into a money making business. The wealthiest Americans were those who owned the land.

It wasn't until the 1920's when mortgages became popular that home ownership gained traction. At that time, only an elite few could qualify for a mortgage and be able to afford to own their own home. After World War II, with the veterans returning home, the government began to issue loans guaranteed by the federal government, and the United States began to experience a housing boom. Veterans were able to get mortgages with no money down, and with the onset of the baby boom, they needed a place for their families.

According to "The History of Home Ownership" which appeared in the Cleveland Plain Dealer in 2008, only 4 out of 10 Americans owned a home in the 1920s. The price for a home in the suburbs of Cleveland at the time was $6,600.

Interestingly enough, I recently saw, on the Internet, the price of housing in those same Cleveland suburbs today is again at $7,000! According to the article, the interest rate on the loan was 6% and the mortgage was financed for 5 years. At the time, the bank required 50% down. In the 1930's, as a result of the Great Depression, the government began to promote home buying to move the economy forward.

Immigration also played a large part in the home ownership game. Thousands of people have come to the United States with the vision of getting a piece of the American pie. The easiest way to get a piece of the pie is to become a home owner. To an immigrant, home ownership represented stability and acceptance into the United States culture. This, too, fueled the home ownership fire and everyone wanted to own a piece of the American dream. It was a good way to be accepted and looked upon as a true citizen of the United States.

Today, most people living in America have bought into the notion that *everyone* needs to own a home. Frequently, I hear people say it is stupid to pay someone else's mortgage as a renter. They say it is throwing money away and you won't recoup the money you have spent on a rental property. However, as a result of the falling real estate prices and the problems which come with home ownership, renting is becoming a more attractive option to many citizens. There are virtually no historical rights and privileges given to a home owner that are not given to everyone else. People who rent can vote, they can run for political office, they can work anywhere they desire and they can live anywhere they want. So the need to own a home to participate in politics and the political process is no longer an issue.

In today's economy, building and buying homes fuel the economy on all levels. It promotes jobs and helps to employ everyone from the foundation builder to the real estate agent. The property taxes paid by home owners also keeps the local governments functioning. In recent years, we have seen school districts close schools because of a diminishing tax base from housing foreclosures. The common school of thought today is that ownership is still a smart investment over the long term. However, this question comes to mind, "Is home ownership for the majority of working, middle class citizens a good investment?"

Summary

- What worked for our founding fathers in the past, may not be acceptable today.

- The rights and privileges given to land owners in the past are extended to everyone today.
- In today's economy, renting is a viable option to home ownership.

Chapter 5

Psychology of Home Ownership

As an American, I can remember people telling me I needed to own a home from the time I could understand money. At the time, it seemed like a great idea. In fact in the mid-80s, it was a great idea to own a home as it was still a great investment. Today, many people still believe owning a home is a great investment. I can recall a recent conversation with a colleague about my book. I shared with her that I was writing a book about the pitfalls of home ownership and I wanted her to contribute. She told me she did not agree with my stance of home ownership possibly not being a good investment and she was not willing to contribute.

"Why not?" I asked.

"Because I believe everyone should own their own home," she replied.

"Why do you believe this?" I asked.

"Because it allows you to leave a legacy for your children." She said.

I replied," Leaving a home as a legacy for your children may not be the wisest decision."
I swear she looked at me like I had two heads. "Listen," I said, "In today's society children are no longer living where they were raised, therefore it may be in their best interest for them to receive a life insurance legacy versus a house. Life insurance benefits pass to your children tax-free where a home creates a tax burden, not to mention the burden of having to sell the property if no one is interested in living in it." I have also seen where having a property can tear a family apart because one person wants to keep it and the other wants to sell it." What was interesting about this conversation is that as we were talking, she was typing an eviction notice for one of her tenants.

"I hate to evict people. This is the part of owning real estate I really hate," she said.

In the words of the late night talk show host Arsenio Hall, it's one of those moments that make you go, "hmmm."

So where did this prevailing attitude that 'we all have to own a home,' come from? Well, as discussed in the previous chapter when we discovered the history of home ownership and the value our founding fathers put on land ownership, we understand why it was so important back in the early centuries. But what about today? Is it still important for all Americans to own a home? Is it still a great investment? There are segments of our society that believe children whose parents own their home are smarter and more well-balanced than children whose parents rent.

In a document titled the <u>Social Consequence of Home ownership</u>, Robert D. Dietz of Ohio State University Department of Economics wrote, "the positive impacts with respect to home ownership are household stability, social involvement, local political participation and activism, environmental awareness, child outcomes, health, and crime reduction." I would like to address some of these social consequences brought out by Dr. Dietz. With respect to household stability, I agree it seems like owning a home would create a more stable home environment. In general, however, as we all know, our country suffers from a 50% divorce rate. The reason cited for these divorces more often than not is financial. The very thing which was supposed to create household stability factors into the instability of the American family. I know, for me, the financial strain of owning our home and other properties caused the demise of my 18 year marriage. This statement of proposed stability also suggests that those who rent instead of buying are unstable, which in my experience is far from the truth.

The next point Dr. Dietz brings out is social involvement. I agree that in the 60s and 70s when families were less mobile and mothers did not work, there was more social involvement on the community level. However, today most of us do not even interact with our neighbors anymore. I remember a time when our neighbors were like a second family. They had the right to discipline us and they had a close, neighborly relationship with our family. But today, with everyone being so busy, neighbors do not get involved with one another and certainly do not discipline each other's children. So the argument for social involvement doesn't stand up any longer.

I do agree with Dr. Dietz that those who own their homes tend to be more politically involved on a local level in their communities. The reason for this is because they are taxpayers and they tend to take a more active stance in the local politics since they have a vested interest in what happens in the community. This is not to say that people who rent do not take a political stand. It also stands to reason that all home owners are not politically involved in their community. Political involvement is a personal choice regardless of home ownership status.

The last area I would like to address which was identified by Dr. Dietz is child outcomes. Dr. Dietz states, "home owners are more likely to monitor and correct socially deviant behavior of children, and perhaps more importantly, adolescents. Also note the stability impact of the status of home ownership creates a positive atmosphere for the developmental maturity of children." Unfortunately, often in today's society, adolescent behavior is reprehensible regardless of home ownership. The Columbine incident is a prime example of this. Again, because of our mobile society, single parent homes, and both parents working coupled with the fact that our neighbors typically don't get involved with each other's families, our children are often left without accountability and tend to act out with or without communal support. The other argument I have heard in favor of home ownership is property values decrease when there are more renters in a neighborhood. Conceivably, this perception can be true. As a renter, I am less likely to invest in the landscape of the property for improvements. I do what is necessary to maintain the property in a neat and orderly fashion but I am not interested in gardening and beautifying the property, so, while the property is neat and clean, it is not cosmetically attractive. I spent thousands of dollars on beautifying the landscape of the property in Florida. Those were thousands of dollars I could have invested in other areas instead of getting into debt. This is an area of maintenance a renter does not have to worry about.

So what about the "us" versus "them" mentality when it comes to home owners versus renters? In some communities there have been all out neighborhood "wars" of home owners versus renters. In our society, renters are sometimes treated as second-class citizens. What is this really about? Perhaps the perception comes from renters being more transient than home owners. Perhaps it is felt renters make less money than home owners and renters have a less caring attitude when it comes to community and politics. Whatever these stereotypes are, they need to be removed from our thought process.

There is a prevailing notion in our society today where home owners are perceived to be smarter with their money than renters. This is because society believes a renter is throwing their money away by paying the landlord's mortgage versus investing in something which belongs to them long-term. Most people who believe this have not done a true examination of the cost of renting versus buying. This thought process is something which has been handed down from generation to generation without numerical proof. This is not to say that everyone who is a renter is smart with their money or everyone who is a home buyer is smart with their money. Every individual situation should be a family decision, without the typical psychological factors influencing their decisions. If an individual chooses to rent, it should be their choice without anyone adversely judging them and making the assumption they are not sensible with their money. It should be noted that the financially savvy person would crunch the numbers before making a decision. For myself personally, I have run the numbers, and for me it makes more sense to rent and invest the rest for the long-term. For the amount of rent I am paying versus the amount of prestige I garner from friends, I would rather spend my money based on what best fits my economical goals. It is in my favor to rent. As a financially savvy person, I would then take the money I save from renting and invest it in my retirement or other financial vehicles for my future.

The point is, we should not be pressured by our friends and family into purchasing a home because everyone else is doing it.

Summary:

- Home ownership does not guarantee you will have a better community. Your children can be well rounded and successful even if you rent rather than buy.

- Home owners are not necessarily smarter with their money. Renters who rent and invest the rest can possibly obtain more financial success than a home owner.
- Don't believe the hype! Home ownership is not necessarily better than renting, investigate for yourself.
- Rent is not a four letter word, it's okay to rent and be proud!

Chapter 6

The Real Cost of Ownership

Determining where you are financially is critical to your decision to rent or buy. Before making that decision, it is recommended that you do a financial analysis. When doing an analysis of the financial feasibility of purchasing a home, a potential buyer must consider all of the costs. The following items are what must be considered in the real cost of home ownership:

- The price of the home
- The down payment
- The interest rate
- The home owner association fees
- Taxes
- Maintenance
- Insurance
- Closing costs

Price

When buying a house you must evaluate its price in comparison to the prices of other homes in the area. A seller will try to get the maximum price for their home and sometimes will inflate the price relative to the houses in the surrounding area. So the first thing to do is to visit other homes which are comparable the same area. Ideally, you should purchase a home which is 20% below the area value. This will get you instant equity in the property to cover some of the initial expenses.

Down Payment

The typical down payment for a FHA conventional loan is 3.5%. On a $250,000 home, the down payment would be $8,750. Some loans require a 20% down payment. On a $250,000 loan it would be $50,000 down. If you put down $50,000 on a house, always consider how long will it take you to recover the cash.

Interest Rates

The interest rate you pay on a loan can have a significant impact on your monthly payment. Typically, the higher your credit scores the better interest rate you can receive. For every additional percent added to your interest rate your payment will increase. It is important to note when you initially begin to pay your mortgage, most of your payment goes towards interest first. It takes approximately 7 years to begin to see the principal go down.

Taxes

Two things are certain in life, death and taxes. As a home owner you are responsible for property taxes. These property taxes also include school, city and county taxes. These taxes are assessed whether you have a child in school or not or whether you use the services of the governmental entities or not. It is interesting to note the tax rate differs all over the United States but on average as a home owner you can expect to pay 3% to 5% of the assessed value of your home for your property taxes. Of course, some areas are lower and others may be higher. There are also certain areas which allow homestead exemptions. This means if you live in the home as your primary residence you can receive a discount on the taxes. Most property tax authorities also give a discount for seniors and disabled owners. When thinking about being a home owner it is important to note that we really do not own the property, the government does. If the taxes are not paid, a lien will be placed on the property and it can be sold for the cost of the tax lien. This can happen even if the mortgage is paid off. What a racket! So while we think we are home owners, the truth is the government owns our homes.

Maintenance

Maintaining a home is one of the biggest expenses of home ownership. If you buy a fixer upper, the cost to renovate can grow into the tens of thousands of dollars before you know it. Routine maintenance such as landscaping, plumbing, painting and other general projects add up over time. As a renter you could possibly be responsible for lawn maintenance but all other maintenance issues fall on the landlord. When we first moved into our rental property, the landlord had to repair the plumbing, paint, replace the garbage disposal and the washer and dryer and a host of other small projects. The total cost was approximately $2,500. Our deposit was $1,100 so from the beginning the landlord was operating at a loss. A month later the upstairs air-conditioning unit went out. The replacement unit costs over $3,000 to replace. If we had purchased this home all of these maintenance issues would have been our expense. How relieved we were to be renters!

When I purchased my home in Florida it was brand new so maintenance was not an immediate issue. However, we spent over $10,000 making the home our own. The largest initial expense was window coverings. Then we painted the entire house. Of course, we had to have new furniture and decorations and all of these things added up.

Many people want to own a home because it gives them the freedom to decorate the way they want. This reason is often cited as a good reason to buy a home. Today, many landlords are reasonable in allowing the renter to decorate their homes. At my last rental house I painted the walls and when I moved out I repainted them white. This allowed me to receive a refund of my entire security deposit. Although I had the option of paying $450 to leave them painted. The other thing to consider is many rental properties are already decorated. Sometimes the home owners must move out, perhaps because of job relocation, and they have invested in fixing up the property. Do not assume because the property is a rental it is not aesthetically appealing. As a former landlord, I appreciated it when my tenants wanted to decorate using their own style. This indicated that they may stay for a longer period of time and also that they cared about the appearance of their home. So if you are a renter with a flair for decorating, ask your landlord if they would mind if you did minor decorations; in most cases they probably will not.

When calculating the cost of maintenance, whether you are buying an existing home or a new home, you may want to figure 1 to 3% of the purchase price. The cost of maintenance over time must also be calculated into the 'buy or not to buy' equation.

Insurance

If there is a mortgage on the property then the mortgage company demands you cover the cost of the property with home owners insurance. As a renter it is up to your discretion as to whether you want to purchase renters insurance. The cost of home owners insurance is approximately 1% to 3% of the home value. The cost of renter's insurance is usually between $400-$700 a year depending on the amount of coverage selected and the area where you live. In Florida, home owner's insurance was several thousand dollars. Most home owner's insurance does not cover flood damage, which would be an additional policy to the home owner's policy. Flood insurance ranges from approximately $400-$1,000 a year. Flood insurance is typically optional, unless you are in a highly flood prone area. Then it may be an additional requirement of your mortgage company.

Taxes and insurance can be included in the monthly mortgage note and are usually known as escrow. Often home owners forget to count the cost of insurance and taxes since they are included in the monthly payment. However, taxes and insurance make up a significant portion of the cost of owning a home.

To Buy or Not to Buy

There is a great calculator on the New York Times website (http://www.nytimes.com/interactive/business/buy-rent-calculator.html). This calculator allows you to determine the breakeven point for home buying versus renting. When I plugged in the numbers for my situation, the calculator determined in 30 years I would not break even by buying a home. (See Figure 1) According to the calculator, I would save approximately $7,000 a year by renting. If I were to save $7,000 a year, with 3% annual increase, at an average return of 6% (which is lower than the stock market average), at the end of 30 years I would have approximately $625,000 (see Figure 2). The question is, "Will my home value appreciate as much in the 30 year period?" So if I stay in the home for 30 years, (which most people do not do any more), I must have the discipline to save this amount in order to reap the benefits, but if I do, my gains could grow significantly.

In order for me to have a better outcome I would have to purchase a home worth $100,000 in order for me to break even in two years. So the question becomes do I want to live in a home worth $100,000? The answer is probably not. A home of this price would not be the size or style of my preference or located in a neighborhood I would want to live in. Therefore, for me it's better to rent in the neighborhood I prefer to live in than to purchase a cheaper house in an area I don't want to live in. What's interesting about this analysis is my income level and housing price point meets middle class America's standards, therefore my scenario is not unusual. Most definitely it would not be worth it to purchase a house greater than $250,000.

An American Nightmare: The Pitfalls of Home Ownership

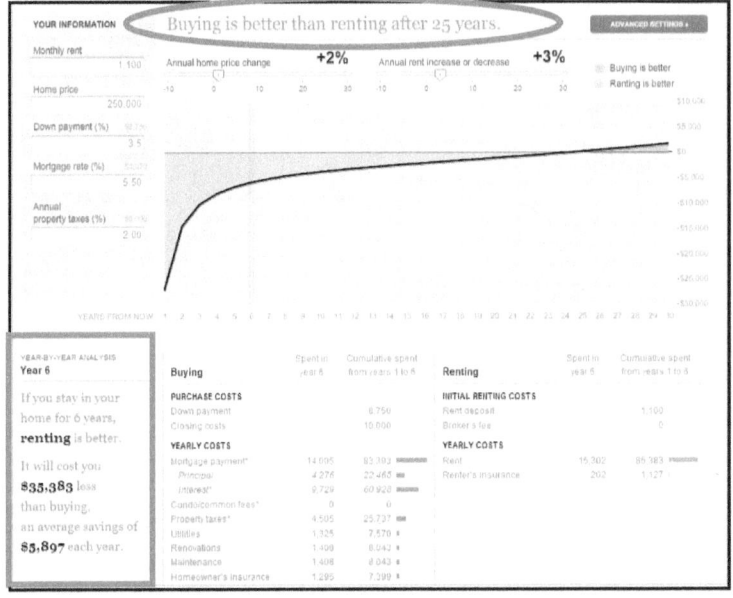

Figure 1

A second scenario proved the opposite is true. My friend is currently renting a home for $2,500 per month (not the best financial move, but she wanted to see what it would be like to live in her dream home). Now, she is considering buying a home. The question is how much home can she buy and will it be worth the money? Let's run the calculator for her scenario:

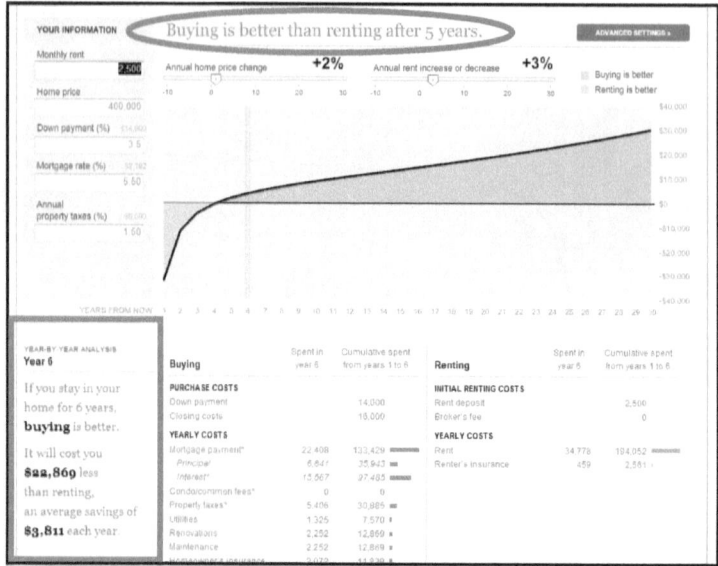

Figure 2

So as you can see after 5 years with a $2,500 per month rent payment it would be in her best interest to buy. However, she does not want to buy a $400,000 house. The upkeep of a house this large will be too much. Now let's take a look at the calculator if she decides to buy a $250,000 home.

An American Nightmare: The Pitfalls of Home Ownership

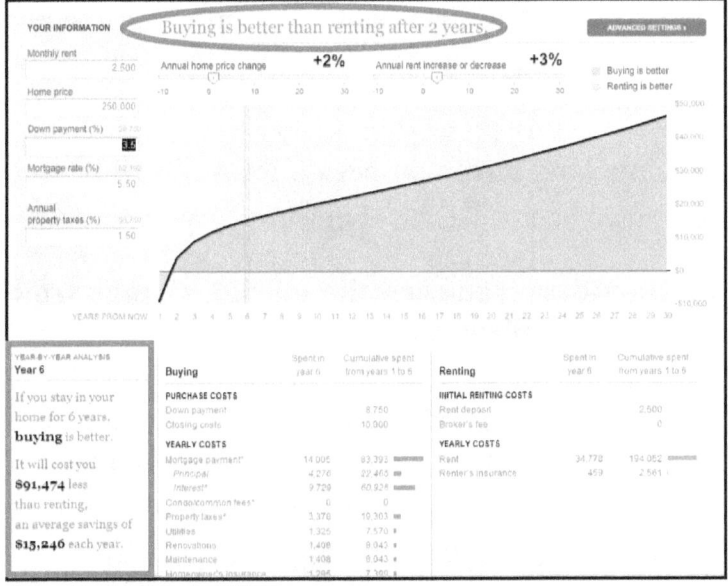

Figure 3

Now my friend is in a better decision making mode as a result of her assessing the pros and cons of home ownership. I encourage everyone to run the calculator to examine your buy vs. renting scenario.

Ask a Realtor

When preparing for this book I spoke to several realtors to get their viewpoint on the concept. Most of the realtors were in agreement; the average buyer had no idea of all of the costs associated with home ownership. One realtor in particular, Godiva Anderson, had this to say about the real estate market:

Q. How long have you been a REALTOR®?

A. I have been a REALTOR® for 13 years.

Q. How have you seen the market change from the early 2000's until now?

A. Since I entered into the real estate profession, I have seen the market change a lot. It was a seller's market, then a buyer's market, and now it is a renter's, buyer's and investor's market.

Q. What are some of the unrealized costs associated with home ownership?

A. Some of the unrealized costs include changes in the tax code for the county or parish where the property is located. The Homeowner's association can vote for increase of dues and or an assessment to pay for various services for the community at any time. Property values decreasing in the subdivision which affect every property and the ability to resell at their asking price. Some of the additional costs are a change in tax exemptions for the home owner. An illness or death in the family which results in a loss of income. The increase in cost of flood and home owner's insurance. Also, not having an escrow account attached to your mortgage payment can cause a tax lien for nonpayment (due to not saving). In addition, the home owners underestimate the cost of routine maintenance.

Q. How do you help a prospective buyer understand the real costs of home ownership?

A. Whether the client is a first time home buyer or a move up, I encourage them to attend a certified home ownership class. The additional education will enhance their knowledge of what I have shared as their REALTOR®. If there are repairs needed, I make sure the seller will pay for the repairs or the buyer has the extra capital instead of borrowing it with the mortgage payment.

Q. What are some of the "aha" moments for the buyers after they have been in the house for a year?

A. "I wished I would have put more than 3% down." Some realize they could have saved the cost of Private Mortgage Insurance (PMI) by putting down 20% or more. Some wished they would have had 6-8 months of reserved savings. They also realize they should not have purchased the new car before or after buying a home. Lastly, some wish they would not have any other debt before and since the closing of their home.

It's important to ask your realtor these questions before purchasing a home. Do your own research and know what your responsibilities are before making a final decision.

Summary

- Before purchasing a home, do your homework.
- How much are the taxes?
- How much is the home insurance?
- Do you need flood insurance?
- How much are the homeowner's association fees?
- What are the rules associated with the home owner's association fees?
- What's your budget for renovations or enhancements?
- Run a cost analysis online to see if you should buy or not.

Chapter 7

Understanding Mortgages

A mortgage truly is a debt for a lifetime. When signing a mortgage you are committing to pay a company for up to 30 years. For many people this is a lifetime. So when signing something for a 30 year commitment, it's important to know exactly what you are getting into. On average we stay in our homes 7 to 10 years. Rarely in today's society do people live in their homes for 30 years. Therefore, when considering buying a home, one of the considerations is how long will you live in the home. It is important to consider your lifestyle, job opportunities, school situation, and growth of your family when committing to a mortgage. If you have a job which will cause you to relocate every few years, then home ownership may not be the way for you to go. This is especially true if your company does not have a home buyout program. Many people purchase a starter home thinking as their family grows they will relocate to a larger home. However, when deciding to buy a home, it is wiser to select your home carefully with a long-term view in mind. As we learned in the previous chapter, when deciding to buy or not to buy, a breakeven point may be 6 to 7 years in the future and buying a starter home may not be a wise decision. As many of us are aware, in 2007 we began to see a rate change in the mortgage industry. Prior to 2007 a family could get a mortgage with no money down purchasing a home five times their income. Hundreds of thousands of those homes went into foreclosure. As a result, the mortgage industry has changed dramatically.

Ask a Mortgage Broker

Purchasing a home can be an emotional decision. After shopping for a home for a period of time and finally locating the ideal home it becomes a very exciting time for the home buyer. Take it from me and my personal experience, those emotions can control your rational thinking, if you let them, when it comes to making financial decisions about your purchase. I have asked a mortgage broker, Shantel Landry, to offer her expertise on mortgages and the current mortgage environment so you can make a level headed decision when deciding to enter into a mortgage.

An American Nightmare: The Pitfalls of Home Ownership

Q. When it comes to mortgages, what are some of the little-known facts the average person needs to know?

A. They need to know everything in the contract. They need to know the financing, the taxes, the insurance and all of those details. All of these things are part of their monthly payment. It is good for the buyer to get preapproved before they start to look for a home. This way they know what they can afford before they fall in love with a house outside of their price range. The mortgage broker can estimate the costs for taxes, insurance, home owner association fees, etc. The mortgage broker can also do a title search to make sure no one else is listed on the title. The buyer might want to get an independent appraiser to make sure the seller is asking a fair price according to comparable properties in the area.

Q. What is a "point" on a loan?

A. Points allow the buyer to buy down the interest rate up front. It is buying down the interest rate for the life of the loan. For instance, if the loan is $150,000 and you purchased 1 point, you would lower the interest by $1,500. So this way, you are not paying the interest during the life of the loan, you are paying it up front. So instead of paying 7%

you are now paying 6% for the life of the loan. This saves interest in the long term.

Q. What is the difference between the various loan types?
A. **<u>FHA</u>**

These mortgages are government backed mortgages. The bank will fund the loan but the government backs the mortgage in case of default. The requirements are typically less strict than a private home lender such as a bank. In order to qualify for an FHA loan the buyer must have 3 to 4 months gross income in a savings account as well as 3½% of the purchasing price as a down payment. For a family who wants to purchase a $250,000 home and is making $150,000 gross income per year, the amount in savings must be $37,500 and the down payment would be $8,750. You must have a total of $46,250 before you can qualify for the loan. For the average family who has children and obligations this is a hefty sum of money to come up with to qualify for the loan.

<u>Conventional</u>

Conventional loans are private loans typically given by banks. The requirements to qualify are very strict and the down payment is approximately

20% of the purchase price and at least 3 months of gross income in savings. Needless to say, most people do not attempt to get a conventional loan unless they are using the property for investment purposes. As a result of the stiffer qualifications, conventional loans are rarely used today for primary residence.

Fixed

A fixed mortgage is one where the interest rate stays the same for the length of the loan. Fixed rate mortgages allow your mortgage payment to be predictable for the duration of the loan. The principal and interest payment will not change during the duration of the loan. This is an advantage over renting because the rental rates are subject to the current market. Therefore, the house renting for $1,000 a month today could easily rent for $1,300 per month five years from now. Conversely, it could also rent for $700 a month. The instability of the rental market could be a reason to consider a mortgage. Most mortgages allow the owner to prepay the loan with little to no penalty. Therefore if a buyer takes a 30-year fixed mortgage they could actually pay it off sooner by adding an additional principal payment on a consistent basis. This allows the home owner to build equity much faster. The problem is, most home owners do not prepay their loan.

Adjustable rate (ARM) or variable mortgages

An adjustable rate mortgage is one where the interest rate can increase or decrease according to the prime market rates. The advantage of this type of loan is the payment could decrease if the interest rates go down. The opposite is also true. If interest rates increase, the mortgage payment can increase as well. In 2007 we saw a dramatic increase in interest rates and many homes went into foreclosure because the owners could not afford the increase in mortgage. The typical ARM loan has a ceiling and a floor. This type of loan is very risky, especially for the home owner who has income which has not increased proportionately. ARM mortgages can be refinanced at a certain period of time, however, you must meet the credit requirements of refinancing. This loan could be beneficial for someone who did not plan to stay in their home long-term. But as we have already mentioned, for someone who will not be in their home long-term renting may be the best option.

Interest rates

The interest we pay on a mortgage is the payment to the lender for lending us their money. Over time the interest can add up considerably. The graphic image on the following pages shows the anatomy of an amortization schedule. This is where you can see the actual interest paid to the lender over the length of the loan. Sometimes this number can be equal to the price of the home! Is it worth it to you to pay the lender the interest you could have kept and invested for yourself. The other important item to note is when paying a monthly mortgage payment most of the payment goes towards interest. It takes 17 years for ½ of the payment to be applied to the principal! (see Figure 4) Strong consideration should be given to whether you want to buy if you are not going to live in your home for a lengthy period of time. If this is the case then it is best to consider renting as your option.

MORTGAGE CALCULATOR
Date: July 1, 2011

Presented by

INTRODUCTION

The loan amount, the interest rate, and the term of the mortgage can have a dramatic effect on the total amount you will eventually pay for the property. Further, mortgage payments typically will include monthly allocations of property taxes, hazard insurance, and (if applicable) private mortgage insurance (PMI). See the impact of these variables along with an amortizaton schedule.

ANALYSIS

Your estimated monthly payments are $1,670.46 (including taxes, insurance, and PMI if applicable), and you will pay $224,980 in interest over the life of the loan.

Loan Information

Loan amount	$241,250
Annual interest rate	5%
Number of months	360
Monthly principal and interest payment	$1,296.08
Monthly property taxes	$208.33
Monthly hazard insurance	$62.50
Monthly PMI (if applicable)	$104.54
Total monthly payment (including taxes, insurance, and PMI)	$1,670.46

If you pay off your house in 30 years, this is the amount you will pay in interest. Do you think you will recover all the interest, maintenance, insurance, and HOA fees paid over 30 years when the home is sold? Not likely.

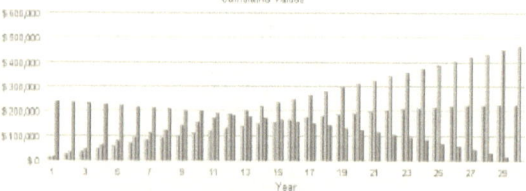

Cumulative Values

Year	Beginning Balance	Interest	Payment	Ending Balance
1	$241,250	$11,982	$15,541	$237,691
2	237,691	11,800	15,541	233,949
3	233,949	11,608	15,541	230,016
4	230,016	11,407	15,541	225,882
5	225,882	11,195	15,541	221,537
6	221,537	10,973	15,541	216,969
7	216,969	10,739	15,541	212,167
8	212,167	10,494	15,541	207,120
9	207,120	10,236	15,541	201,815
10	201,815	9,964	15,541	196,238
11	196,238	9,679	15,541	190,375

An American Nightmare: The Pitfalls of Home Ownership

12	190,375	9,379	15,541	184,213
13	184,213	9,064	15,541	177,736
14	177,736	8,732	15,541	170,927
15	170,927	8,384	15,541	163,770
16	163,770	8,018	15,541	156,247
17	156,247	7,633	15,541	148,338
18	148,338	7,228	15,541	140,025
19	140,025	6,803	15,541	131,287
20	131,287	6,356	15,541	122,102
21	122,102	5,886	15,541	112,447
22	112,447	5,392	15,541	102,298
23	102,298	4,873	15,541	91,629
24	91,629	4,327	15,541	80,415
25	80,415	3,753	15,541	68,627
26	68,627	3,150	15,541	56,236
27	56,236	2,516	15,541	43,211
28	43,211	1,850	15,541	29,520
29	29,520	1,149	15,541	15,128
30	$15,128	$413	$15,541	$0

It takes 17 years for more than ½ your payment to go towards the principal balance. By then you would have paid more than $92,000 in interest!

SUMMARY OF INPUT

Loan amount	$241,250
Annual interest rate	5.00%
Number of months. (30yrs=360)	360
Desired amortization schedule	yearly
Sale price of property	$250,000
Let system estimate property taxes, insurance, and private mortgage insurance? If No then detail	Yes
Annual property taxes	$0
Annual hazard insurance	$0
Monthly private mortgage insurance	$0

Q. What tips would you give new home buyers?

A. Shop for the lowest interest rate possible. Make sure they can afford the home. Do a budget for the long-term.

Q. What's an origination fee and how is it assessed?

A. The origination fee is the percentage a broker is paid. This fee is typically paid by the buyer. The current market is paying 1% point to the mortgage broker, however, the broker can legally charge up to 3%. The fee should be assessed on the circumstances of the loan.

Q. What's your opinion on whether home buying vs. renting is a good investment for middle income Americans?

A. It depends on the cost of living. Something the home buyer has to consider are taxes, homeowner insurance, association fees and maintenance.

When determining whether or not to take out a mortgage, it is very important that all things are considered. The most important factors are the length of the loan, the amount of time you are going to spend in the home, the interest rate, and the type of loan. It is also very important that you shop to get the best interest rates and lowest origination fee possible for your situation.

Summary

- Before taking out a mortgage, examine the amount of time you will be in the home.
- Get preapproved to make sure you can afford the home.
- Save three months income in a savings account along with your down payment.
- Consider the type of loan which is best for your financial situation and lifestyle.

Chapter 8

Solutions

There are many advantages and disadvantages to renting versus home buying. We will examine a few of them here for you to decide for yourself if buying a home or renting is right for you. Let's take a look at buying a home. Some of the advantages of being a home owner is conceivably your property should build equity, although since 2007 we have seen many homes are upside down. This is where the remaining balance on the mortgage is more than the price you could get if you sell the home. My mother and I were actually talking about this fact recently and said the term upside down used to only be associated with a car. This is when it became apparent a car was no longer a good investment. In fact she stated she was upside down in her home. She would love to move to a senior community but cannot sell her home and receive any equity although she has lived there approximately 12 years. She feels trapped. If a mortgage is owed on the property then there may be no equity. If this is the case, the homeowner either stays in the home or sells the home at a loss.

Another advantage of home ownership is the freedom to decorate or make cosmetic upgrades. I hate to turn a perceived advantage into a disadvantage, but we must examine the power of a homeowner's association (HOA). If you live in a community governed by a home owner's association you may not have the freedom to do with your property as you please. When looking for a home it is very important to understand the rules and regulations of the homeowner's association. If you like pink houses, you probably cannot paint your house pink under the rules of a homeowner's association. They have the right to govern what you can and cannot do with "your property." I remember when I lived in Florida, there was a lawsuit between a home owner and a homeowner's association because the home owner wanted to put a commercial style flagpole in his front yard with a large American flag. The homeowner's association said it did not meet their standard guidelines and because he installed it anyway they sued him. The home owner eventually won but only after $75,000 in legal fees, 28 trips to the courthouse and 8½ years later. Wow! So while you believe you own the property, the truth is, you may not be able to control the property. These rules also pertain to building on and adding to your property. All improvements to the outside of the property must be approved by the homeowner's association. If the rules are too stringent, then future buyers of your property may shy away from purchasing in your neighborhood which will make your property hard to sell. The homeowner's association may also have to approve your buyer. And if they don't like the way a person is wearing their hair or the psychedelic shirt they are wearing, they can make up a reason to disapprove them. I have personally seen this myself. My friend Amber was attempting to buy a property and they said she would have too many people living in her home and stalled and delayed on getting her approval until she gave up purchasing the property. As the buyer she was extremely disappointed because she loved the home. While I do not know the seller personally, I know it took a long time for them to get a potential buyer and for the buyer to be disapproved by the home owners association for no good reason was unthinkable. My experience with homeowner's associations were particularly negative in Florida. However, whenever you locate a house that is governed by an HOA, it is very important to review their rules before you fall in love with the home. By the way, we have not discussed how a homeowner's association can charge whatever they want, when they want, if you live in their community. Some of the fees, particularly in Florida, are outrageous! I have heard of home owner's association fees running as much as $3,000 or more per year. This is an additional $250 a month out of your household budget. What are you getting for this fee? Look very, very closely at homeowner's associations before making a decision on the home. On the other hand, the positive side to a homeowner's association is they typically keep the neighborhood looking well. They don't allow things like junk cars in yards, crazy color paint on homes and the bad elements to move into the neighborhood.

Another advantage of home ownership is the ability to write off your mortgage interest and property taxes. This is the most declared advantage to buying a home. Somehow people get stuck on the fact you can deduct interest and property taxes on your income taxes. But what they don't understand is 1) it is not a dollar for dollar deduction, it is an income reduction which may or may not change your tax bracket, and 2) if you didn't have to pay them there would be nothing to deduct. One hundred percent of those funds would be available for your personal use. The other big factor which is often not considered when deciding to purchase a home is how much home do I have to buy to make the tax deduction worth it. For instance in my analysis of whether I should buy or not, it said I should purchase a $100,000 home. When looking at the amount of property taxes and interest I will pay on $100,000 home, this amount will not be greater than the standard deduction allowed on federal taxes. In other words it's more to my advantage to take the free standard deduction then to pay property taxes and interest on $100,000 mortgage. The bottom line is you should review your tax situation to see if the amount of home you are purchasing will give you a "real" tax break.

Ask a Tax Expert

I have requested my tax consultant, Karla Dennis, to give us her perspective on home ownership as it relates to taxes.

Q. When it comes to taxes and home ownership, what items are tax deductible to a home owner only? Are property upgrades deductible?

A. When it comes to home ownership, the only items which are tax deductible to the home owner is the mortgage interest and the property taxes. If this is a new purchase, the home owner will also be able to deduct the points paid upfront on the loan. Unfortunately, upgrades are not tax deductible unless the person has a home office and only a percentage is tax deductible based on the square footage of the home and the portion used for business. On occasion, there are incentive tax credits a home owner can get for upgrading their appliances to lower energy usage but this is not always the case. Laws which motivate home owners to complete certain upgrades to their home are only cyclical and are not available all the time.

Q. How much house does a person have to buy for the deductions above to exceed the standard tax deduction? In other words, if a person buys a house for $50,000 (which can still be done in Houston) the taxes and interest paid won't exceed the standard deduction so the ability to deduct those items is moot, right?

A. Mortgage interest is deductible regardless of the amount you are paying. The key is whether or not you should bother deducting the mortgage interest, taxes and other itemized deductions if they are not going to exceed the standard deduction. The standard deduction changes a bit every year and varies depending on if you are married filing jointly, married filing separately, single, or head of household. The deduction for 2011 varies from $11,600 down to $5,800. Unless, you can deduct the mortgage interest amount over the standard deduction, it may not make sense to only buy a house for tax deduction purposes. You really have to evaluate the numbers and see if the deduction of the interest and property taxes puts you in a better tax position.

Q. Tax and interest deductions are not dollar-for-dollar. Approximately, what percentage of the total taxes and interest paid are really deductible?

A. Tax and interest deductions are exactly what they are: deductions against income. Many taxpayers think if they buy a property they are getting back the amount they are paying in interest and property taxes. This is not true. If you make $75,000 per year in wages as earnings, and the taxes and interest you paid all year is $25,000, you are going to pay tax on the $50,000 per year, which is the difference between $75,000 as earnings and $25,000 in interest. This deduction allows you to drop into a lower income tax bracket. Instead of being taxed at 27%, you may be taxed at 15%. For simplicity sake, this example does not take into consideration other deductions the taxpayers are allowed to have, but it clearly demonstrates in the simplest form how the mortgage interest is treated for tax purposes.

Q. How do tax deductions from a home based business work? I think it's a percentage of the space used. Also, a renter can deduct home based business expenses too, right?

A. Tax deductions for a home based business are a joke in my opinion. First of all, if you own a home, chances are you are already deducting your mortgage interest and property taxes. A home based business allocation allows you to deduct a percentage of the mortgage interests and property taxes specifically against the income of the business. If your home is 1,000 square feet and the home office is 100 square feet, and then you are able to deduct 10% of your expenses of operating your home against the net profit from the business. The key is for the business to have net profit. If it does not have net profit then your home office deductions are not allowed until the business makes a profit. In addition to deducting mortgage interest and property taxes against your net profit, you can also deduct a percentage of the utilities and other expenses you have in operating your home. Another important key ingredient is the home office must be a separate room used exclusively for business. Thus, if you are surfing the internet for personal usage or paying household bills in your home office then according to IRS guidelines it is not tax deductible.

Q. Are there any little known "out of the box" tax provisions a renter can take advantage of (like deductions for a home business)?

A. The renter gets the bigger advantage of a home office. The reason is the renter cannot deduct their rent on their tax return. If they have a home office, they are getting to deduct a percentage of their rent which would normally not be deductible. The deduction is still only a percentage of the total square footage but most rental units are a lot less square footage than an entire house.

Again, doing your homework and running the numbers before you decide to buy a home and how much home to buy is very important.

A huge advantage to owning a home is that the principal and interest payments on your mortgage are level throughout the duration of the mortgage. The only fluctuation you may experience is if the property taxes and insurance increase significantly and those payments are built into your mortgage payments through escrow. I experienced this when we lived in Florida and we went through the boom in house prices. Our escrow payments increased by $600 per month! We certainly were not prepared to pay an additional $600 a month just because the housing market had increased. I had to come up with $3,000 to avoid an increased mortgage payment. This was a rude awakening. As a renter you may be subject to rental price increases on an annual basis. Fortunately most owners don't increase rental prices often; however, it could happen. Certainly a rental increase of $600 a month is not likely to happen. If it does, you can move. However, when my escrow payment increased I was not free to move because I was a home owner. Therein lies another difference between being a home owner and a renter.

The Advantages to Renting

The advantages to renting are great. The primary advantage is the freedom from being tied down to a mortgage and a house. One of the reasons I like to rent is because of my personality. I get bored easily. I like change. Do you rush to buy a home if you are the type of person who knows you will not live in the same house or neighborhood for 30 years? Then renting may be more of your preference. The longest I have stayed in a house is nine years, which was the first house we purchased and I described at the beginning of the book. Renters are free to come and go as they please. If the neighborhood deteriorates, a renter can move. If they don't like the neighbors they can move. If there are maintenance problems in the house, a renter can move. If they want to try out

An American Nightmare: The Pitfalls of Home Ownership

another area of town, they can move. However, as a home owner if any of these situations arise in most cases you are stuck. When we lived in Florida we had a neighbor from hell. They hung sheets in the windows, had late-night parties and had trash all over their yard. They were renters. But what could we do about it? Nothing. Wait for them to move. But what if your neighbor is a regular home owner like you and they are not an ideal neighbor. You are forced to live next to them for who knows how long. Recently, there was a segment on the news about feuding neighbors which had come to the point where they got violent because of their disagreements. If one of those neighbors were renters, they could move.

The ultimate freedom is the ability to pick up and move whenever you want, preferably the end of your lease term, but if not, all you lose is your security deposit. If you are a home owner, you have to wait until you find a buyer who likes your home, has the down payment, is credit worthy to qualify for a mortgage, and meets the homeowner association's criteria. This process could take months, even years, to find a qualified buyer. If you are in a situation where perhaps your job relocates you and you need to get out of your home quickly, then being a home owner is an additional burden. I know of many situations where home owners had to leave the property vacant because their job required them to move immediately. There used to be a time when corporations would buyout the home owner; however, those times are quickly becoming a thing of the past.

The second advantage to renting is not being responsible for maintenance. When I moved into my latest rental property several things went wrong immediately. I won't list them here but the cost added up to be over $6000. The landlord was responsible for fixing all of the problems, so she started out in the hole. Had we purchased this home, those maintenance problems would have been ours. A home owner can expect to spend about $3,000-$5,000 a year on maintenance. A renter spends $0. A good renter may take care of minor maintenance problems which are less than $100, however, they are not obligated to pay for any maintenance. If the maintenance problems become too much, they can move. By the way, moving is an expensive undertaking so I am not advocating moving on an annual basis, but the point is, a renter has the freedom to move around however they please. I was watching a television program on HGTV where a young couple purchased their first home and had it inspected prior to buying; however, they ended up with a termite infestation which cost them several thousand dollars to get rid of. They were devastated not to mention mortified to have to live with termites. If they were renters this responsibility would have been the landlords.

Rent and Invest the Rest

"Rent" is not a four letter word. It is perfectly okay to be a renter if you are a smart renter. In the past, renting was seen as the ultimate financial mistake, but as we have investigated the pros and cons of both, buying a home could be a mistake for you or your family. We have considered several factors that go into whether renting is a smart money decision. The first factor is how much you are paying for rent. The second factor is how long you intend to rent. The third factor is how much house would you buy? The fourth factor is how long will you live in the house if you buy? Lastly, can I afford taxes, maintenance, insurance, and interest payments on a $250,000 loan? Run the analysis for yourself and see if renting is a better financial decision for you and your family. Let me re-emphasize; the key here is to be a smart renter. If you're not going to build equity in a home, then it is imperative to invest or save the money which would have been spent on the upkeep of the home. Otherwise, you will not be a smart renter, but a broke renter. The easiest way to begin to invest or save the funds you would have spent on the maintenance of a home is by payroll deduction. If your employer will deduct funds and send them to a separate savings account, then it is a great way to start to build a financial nest egg for yourself. If your employer offers a retirement savings plan, you may want to consider participating in their plan fully. You should consult with a financial advisor as to what method is more suitable for you to get started with your savings plan and how to invest the funds. The point is not to spend the money that you're saving on not buying a home; the point is to rent and invest the rest. Below is an illustration, showing the financial possibilities of how your money can grow if you are disciplined and invest the money you are saving from not owning a home. You may also visit the website www.fincalc.com and run your own analysis. Don't forget about the New York Times' website as well to run a "buy or not to buy" analysis. See the reference in Chapter 6 for the exact website location.

An American Nightmare: The Pitfalls of Home Ownership

WHAT COULD MY CURRENT SAVINGS GROW TO?

Date: May 28, 2017

Presented by CalcXML

INTRODUCTION

Compound interest can have a dramatic effect on the growth of series of regular savings and initial lump sum deposits. Use this calculator to determine the future value of your savings and lump sum.

ANALYSIS

Based on your savings schedule, you will accumulate $624,728 over the next 30 years.

Growth Of Savings

Year	Beginning Balance	Savings @ 3.0%	Earnings @ 8.0%	Taxes @ 28.0%	Ending Balance
1	$0	$7,000	$420	$118	$7,302
2	7,302	7,210	871	244	15,139
3	15,139	7,426	1,354	379	23,540
4	23,540	7,649	1,871	524	32,537
5	32,537	7,879	2,425	679	42,161
6	42,161	8,115	3,017	845	52,448
7	52,448	8,358	3,648	1,022	63,434
8	63,434	8,609	4,323	1,210	75,155
9	75,155	8,867	5,041	1,412	87,652
10	87,652	9,133	5,807	1,626	100,967
11	100,967	9,407	6,622	1,854	115,142
12	115,142	9,690	7,490	2,097	130,225
13	130,225	9,980	8,412	2,355	146,262
14	146,262	10,280	9,392	2,630	163,304
15	163,304	10,588	10,434	2,921	181,404
16	181,404	10,906	11,539	3,231	200,618
17	200,618	11,233	12,711	3,559	221,003
18	221,003	11,570	13,954	3,907	242,620
19	242,620	11,917	15,272	4,276	265,533
20	265,533	12,275	16,668	4,667	289,809
21	289,809	12,643	18,147	5,081	315,517
22	315,517	13,022	19,712	5,519	342,732

This information may help you analyze your financial needs. It is based on information and assumptions provided by you regarding your goals, expectations and financial situation. The calculations do not infer that the company assumes any fiduciary duties. The calculations provided should not be construed as financial, legal or tax advice. In addition, such information should not be relied upon as the only source of information. This information is supplied from sources we believe to be reliable but we cannot guarantee its accuracy. Hypothetical illustrations may provide historical or current performance information. Past performance does not guarantee nor indicate future results.

23	342,732	13,413	21,369	5,983	371,531
24	371,531	13,815	23,121	6,474	401,993
25	401,993	14,230	24,973	6,993	434,203
26	434,203	14,656	26,932	7,541	468,250
27	468,250	15,096	29,001	8,120	504,227
28	504,227	15,549	31,187	8,732	542,230
29	542,230	16,015	33,495	9,379	582,362
30	$582,362	$16,496	$35,931	$10,061	$624,728

SUMMARY OF INPUT

Initial balance or deposit	$0
Annual savings amount	$7,000
Annual increase in contributions	3.00%
Number of years for the analysis	30
Before-tax return on savings: (%)	6.00%
Marginal tax bracket: (%)	28.00%

Input parameters

This information may help you analyze your financial needs. It is based on information and assumptions provided by you regarding your goals, expectations and financial situation. The calculations do not infer that the company assumes any fiduciary duties. The calculations provided should not be construed as financial, legal or tax advice. In addition, such information should not be relied upon as the only source of information. This information is supplied from sources we believe to be reliable but we cannot guarantee its accuracy. Hypothetical illustrations may provide historical or current performance information. Past performance does not guarantee nor indicate future results.

In conclusion, it is my desire that you have been challenged by reading this information. I want you to now be able to make an informed decision about:

- Whether this is the right time for you to purchase a home.
- The price point of the home you want to buy to gain the maximum financial benefit.
- The financials of whether home ownership is truly an investment for you.
- Home owner's associations and whether you want to choose a home governed by a HOA.

As our economy continues to recover from its worst housing crisis, it appears that now is a good time to buy a home, and it possibly could be. But don't be fooled, all of the real costs of home ownership still exist no matter when the home is purchased. Remember, a savvy buyer examines a situation from all sides before making a purchase.

Summary

- Understand the rules of your prevailing home owner's association before purchasing a home.
- The tax benefits may not outweigh the costs of owning a home.
- Don't buy a home just for the tax benefits.
- Save the money for your future that would have ordinarily went for the costs of owning a home.

www.ingramcontent.com/pod-product-compliance
Lightning Source LLC
Chambersburg PA
CBHW020453220526
45464CB00002B/977